MASTERING MACD

A Comprehensive Guide to the macd
Indicator in Trading

by

Lalit Mohanty

Table of Contents

PREFACE

In the fast-paced and ever-evolving realm of financial markets, the ability to navigate trends and make informed decisions is the key to success. As traders, we are continually seeking effective tools to decipher market movements and enhance our strategies. This preface serves as an introduction to "Mastering MACD: A Comprehensive Guide to Trading Strategies and Future Trends," a book crafted with the goal of equipping traders with the knowledge and insights needed to master the Moving Average Convergence Divergence (MACD) indicator.

The decision to focus on MACD stems from its universal popularity and effectiveness among traders of various experience levels. Whether you are a seasoned professional or a newcomer to the world of trading, this guide aims to provide valuable insights into the intricacies of MACD and its diverse applications.

As we embark on this journey, it's essential to acknowledge the dynamic nature of financial markets. The tools and strategies that worked yesterday might require adaptation tomorrow. With this in mind, "Mastering MACD" not only delves into the foundational principles of MACD but also explores advanced strategies and considers the future landscape of technical analysis.

This book is structured to cater to different levels of expertise, beginning with the basics and progressively moving towards more complex strategies. Real-world examples, case studies, and practical applications are interwoven to facilitate a comprehensive understanding of how MACD can be effectively employed in various market scenarios.

Moreover, the integration of machine learning, discussions on cryptocurrency trading, and insights into the psychological aspects of trading contribute to the holistic approach of this guide. We recognize that successful trading extends beyond technical analysis; it involves a balance of strategy, discipline, and adaptability.

We invite you to embark on this learning journey with an open mind, ready to absorb the principles, strategies, and future trends that "Mastering MACD" unfolds. Whether you're seeking to refine existing skills, explore new strategies, or simply deepen your understanding of MACD, we believe this guide will serve as a valuable resource in your trading endeavors.

Wishing you success and fulfillment in your trading journey.

CHAPTER 1: INTRODUCTION TO MACD

1.1 Understanding Technical Analysis

In the vast world of financial markets, traders and investors seek tools that can help them make informed decisions about buying or selling assets. Technical analysis is a discipline that involves studying past market data, primarily price and volume, to forecast future price movements. It operates on the premise that historical price movements tend to repeat and leave discernible patterns.

Technical analysts use various indicators and chart patterns to identify trends, reversals, and potential entry or exit points. Among these tools, the Moving Average Convergence Divergence (MACD) stands out as a versatile and widely used indicator, providing insights into the strength and direction of trends.

1.2 The Birth of MACD

Developed by Gerald Appel in the late 1970s, the Moving Average Convergence Divergence (MACD) indicator quickly gained popularity among traders. Appel aimed to create an indicator that could reveal both the speed and direction of a trend, offering a more comprehensive view of market dynamics.

The MACD indicator is derived from the differences between two exponential moving averages (EMAs). By subtracting the longer-term EMA from the shorter-term EMA, the indicator captures the momentum and trend strength. Appel also introduced a signal line, usually a nine-day EMA, to smooth out the MACD line and generate trading signals.

1.3 The Components of MACD

The MACD consists of three main components:

1.3.1 MACD Line (Fast Line)

The MACD Line represents the difference between the 12-day and 26-day exponential moving averages. It reflects short-term momentum and the speed at which a trend is developing. Traders often look for crossovers with the signal line for potential buy or sell signals.

1.3.2 Signal Line (Slow Line)

The Signal Line is a nine-day exponential moving average of the MACD Line. It smoothens the MACD Line, making it easier to identify trends and potential reversals. Crossovers between the MACD Line and the Signal Line generate signals for entering or exiting trades.

1.3.3 Histogram

The Histogram is a visual representation of the difference between the MACD Line and the Signal Line. When the MACD Line is above the Signal Line, the Histogram is positive, indicating bullish momentum. Conversely, a negative Histogram suggests bearish momentum. Histogram bars shrinking or expanding can signal changes in momentum.

Understanding these components is crucial for interpreting MACD charts effectively. In the subsequent chapters, we will delve deeper into the mathematical calculations, strategies, and practical applications of the MACD indicator to empower you in making informed trading decisions.

CHAPTER 2: GETTING STARTED

2.1 Installing and Configuring MACD on Trading Platforms

To harness the power of the Moving Average Convergence Divergence (MACD) indicator, it's essential to integrate it into your preferred trading platform. Most popular trading platforms, such as MetaTrader, TradingView, and Thinkorswim, offer built-in tools for incorporating MACD into your charts.

- **MetaTrader:**

    - Locate the "Indicators" folder in the platform.

    - Find and select MACD from the list of available indicators.

    - Adjust settings such as the fast and slow EMA periods as needed.

    - Apply the indicator to your chart.

- **TradingView:**
    - Open the indicators tab, usually found on the top toolbar.
    - Search for MACD and add it to your chart.
    - Customize the indicator's parameters according to your preferences.

- **Thinkorswim:**
    - Navigate to the "Studies" menu.
    - Choose "Edit Studies."
    - Locate and add MACD from the list.
    - Configure the indicator settings and apply.

Once installed, MACD will be overlaid onto your price chart, providing insights into market momentum and potential trend reversals.

2.2 Interpreting MACD Charts

Understanding MACD charts is fundamental for effective analysis. The three main components – MACD Line, Signal Line, and Histogram – work in tandem to provide valuable information:

- **MACD Line (Fast Line):** Watch for crossovers with the Signal Line. When the MACD Line crosses above the Signal Line, it may signal a bullish trend, while a crossover below could indicate a bearish trend.

- **Signal Line (Slow Line):** Acts as a smoother for the MACD Line. Crossovers with the MACD Line generate buy or sell signals.

- **Histogram:** The visual representation of the difference between the MACD and Signal Lines. Positive bars indicate bullish momentum, and negative bars suggest bearish momentum. Changes in the Histogram's size can indicate shifts in market strength.

2.3 Choosing the Right Timeframe

The timeframe you choose for your MACD analysis is critical. Different timeframes provide distinct perspectives on market trends and can influence the accuracy of signals. Common timeframes include:

- **Short-term (Intraday):** Suitable for day traders seeking quick opportunities.

- **Medium-term (Daily to Weekly):** Preferred by swing traders capturing trends over several days to weeks.

- **Long-term (Monthly):** Suited for investors focusing on overall market trends and macroeconomic factors.

Adapt the MACD settings and interpretation to your chosen timeframe. Shorter periods may generate more signals but may also be noisier, while longer periods may offer more robust signals but with fewer occurrences.

In the following chapters, we will explore various MACD strategies, optimization techniques, and real-world applications to enhance your proficiency in using this powerful indicator.

CHAPTER 3: THE MATHEMATICS BEHIND MACD

3.1 Exponential Moving Averages (EMAs)

At the core of the Moving Average Convergence Divergence (MACD) indicator are Exponential Moving Averages (EMAs). An EMA assigns different weights to each price point, giving more significance to recent data. The formula for calculating an EMA is as follows:

$EMA_t = (Price_t - EMA_{t-1}) \times \text{Multiplier} + EMA_{t-1}$
Where:

- EMA_t is the EMA at time t,

- $Price_t$ is the closing price at time t,

- EMA_{t-1} is the EMA at the previous time period,

- The \text{Multiplier} is calculated as 2/Period+1, with the Period representing the chosen timeframe.

The MACD uses two EMAs, typically a 12-day EMA (short-term) and a 26-day EMA (long-term), to calculate the MACD Line.

3.2 Signal Line Calculations

The Signal Line, a 9-day EMA of the MACD Line, provides a smoothed curve, making it easier to identify trends and potential reversal points. The formula for the Signal Line is similar to that of the MACD Line:

$$Signal_t=(MACD_t-Signal_{t-1})\times Signal\ Multiplier+Signal_{t-1}$$

Where:

- *Signal_t* is the Signal Line at time t,
- *MACD_t* is the MACD Line at time t,
- *Signal_{t-1}* is the Signal Line at the previous time period,
- The \text{Signal Multiplier} is calculated as 2/Signal Period+1, with the Signal Period typically set at 9.

3.3 Histogram and MACD Line

The Histogram represents the difference between the MACD Line and the Signal Line, providing a visual representation of the convergence and divergence between these two components. The Histogram is calculated as follows:

$$Histogram_t = MACD_t - Signal_t$$

Positive values indicate that the MACD Line is above the Signal Line, signaling bullish momentum, while negative values suggest bearish momentum.

The MACD Line itself is the difference between the short-term (12-day) and long-term (26-day) EMAs:

$$MACD\ Line_t = EMA_{12,t} - EMA_{26,t}$$

Understanding the mathematical foundation of MACD is crucial for interpreting its signals and customizing its parameters to suit different trading strategies. In the subsequent chapters, we will explore practical applications, strategies, and advanced techniques to maximize the effectiveness of the MACD indicator in your trading endeavors.

CHAPTER 4: TRADITIONAL MACD STRATEGIES

4.1 Basic MACD Crossovers

One of the most straightforward and widely used strategies involving the Moving Average Convergence Divergence (MACD) indicator is based on crossovers between the MACD Line and the Signal Line. These crossovers signal potential shifts in market momentum and are key entry and exit points for traders.

- **Bullish Crossover (Golden Cross):**
  - Occurs when the MACD Line crosses above the Signal Line.
  - Suggests a potential upward trend.
  - Considered a buy signal.

- **Bearish Crossover (Death Cross):**

    - Occurs when the MACD Line crosses below the Signal Line.

    - Indicates a potential downward trend.

    - Considered a sell signal.

Traders often wait for confirmation from other indicators or price action before acting on crossovers to reduce the risk of false signals.

4.2 Divergence and Convergence

Divergence and convergence refer to the relationship between the price trend and the MACD indicator. These patterns can signal potential trend reversals:

- **Bullish Divergence:**

    - Occurs when the price makes lower lows, but the MACD Histogram makes higher lows.

    - Suggests weakening bearish momentum and potential for a bullish reversal.

- **Bearish Divergence:**

    - Occurs when the price makes higher highs, but the MACD Histogram makes lower highs.

    - Indicates weakening bullish momentum and potential for a bearish reversal.

- **Convergence:**

  - Occurs when the price and MACD Histogram move in the same direction.

  - Can confirm the strength of an existing trend.

Divergence and convergence are powerful tools for anticipating trend shifts, but traders should exercise caution and use additional analysis to validate signals.

4.3 Using MACD to Confirm Trends

In addition to signaling potential reversals, the MACD can be employed to confirm existing trends. This involves aligning the direction of the MACD Line with the overall market trend:

- **Bullish Trend Confirmation:**

  - The MACD Line is above the Signal Line.

  - Both lines are in positive territory.

  - Indicates strong bullish momentum.

- **Bearish Trend Confirmation:**

  - The MACD Line is below the Signal Line.

  - Both lines are in negative territory.

  - Suggests strong bearish momentum.

By confirming trends, traders can strengthen their confidence in the prevailing market direction and make more informed decisions about entering or exiting trades.

These traditional MACD strategies provide a solid foundation for traders. However, it's essential to consider market conditions, incorporate risk management, and be cautious of false signals. In the following chapters, we will explore more advanced strategies and techniques for optimizing the use of MACD in various trading scenarios.

CHAPTER 5: ADVANCED MACD STRATEGIES

5.1 MACD Histogram Patterns

While the MACD Histogram is primarily a visual representation of the difference between the MACD Line and the Signal Line, specific patterns within the Histogram can offer additional insights into market momentum.

- **Twin Peaks:**
  - Indicates a potential trend reversal.
  - Two peaks form above the zero line, with the second lower than the first.
  - Suggests weakening bullish momentum.
- **Divergence/Convergence:**
  - Histogram diverges from the price chart.

- Can signal an impending trend reversal.

- Convergence indicates the strengthening of the existing trend.

- **Zero-Line Reversals:**

  - Crossing the zero line from negative to positive indicates a shift from bearish to bullish momentum.

  - Crossing from positive to negative suggests a shift from bullish to bearish momentum.

Analyzing Histogram patterns can enhance the precision of MACD signals, providing traders with a more nuanced understanding of market dynamics.

5.2 MACD Slope and Momentum

Examining the slope and momentum of the MACD Line itself can offer valuable information about the strength and duration of a trend.

- **Increasing Slope:**

  - A rising MACD Line suggests accelerating momentum in the current trend.

  - Traders may consider adding to existing positions or entering new trades.

- **Decreasing Slope:**

- A declining MACD Line indicates a slowdown in momentum.

- Traders may exercise caution, as a potential trend reversal or consolidation could be imminent.

- **Zero-Line Crossings:**

  - Crossing above the zero line suggests a shift to bullish momentum.

  - Crossing below the zero line indicates a shift to bearish momentum.

Analyzing the slope and momentum of the MACD Line can help traders make more informed decisions about the sustainability of trends and the timing of their trades.

5.3 Combining MACD with Other Indicators

To further refine trading strategies, traders often combine MACD with other technical indicators to gain a more comprehensive view of market conditions.

- **Moving Averages:**

  - Confirm MACD signals with the trend direction indicated by simple or exponential moving averages.

- **Relative Strength Index (RSI):**

- Use RSI in conjunction with MACD to identify overbought or oversold conditions, corroborating potential trend reversals.

- **Bollinger Bands:**

  - Combine Bollinger Bands with MACD to identify volatility and potential breakout or breakdown points.

- **Fibonacci Retracements:**

  - Use Fibonacci levels to identify potential support or resistance levels, confirming MACD signals.

By integrating MACD with other indicators, traders can create more robust and reliable trading strategies. However, it's crucial to understand the strengths and limitations of each indicator and consider the overall market context.

In the following chapters, we will explore practical examples and case studies, providing a deeper understanding of how advanced MACD strategies can be applied in real-world trading scenarios.

CHAPTER 6: PRACTICAL APPLICATION

6.1 Real-world Examples of MACD Trades

To truly grasp the effectiveness of the Moving Average Convergence Divergence (MACD) indicator, examining real-world examples can provide valuable insights into its application.

- **Example 1: Basic MACD Crossover**

    - **Scenario:** A bullish crossover occurs as the MACD Line crosses above the Signal Line.

    - **Action:** Traders might consider entering a long position, anticipating a potential upward trend.

    - **Outcome:** Profitability if the trend continues; caution if other indicators or factors suggest potential reversals.

- **Example 2: Bullish Divergence**

  - **Scenario:** The price makes lower lows, but the MACD Histogram forms higher lows.

  - **Action:** Anticipate a potential bullish reversal.

  - **Outcome:** Profitability if the trend reverses; manage risk with proper position sizing and risk management strategies.

- **Example 3: Zero-Line Reversal**

  - **Scenario:** MACD crosses above the zero line from negative to positive.

  - **Action:** Indication of a shift to bullish momentum.

  - **Outcome:** Consider entering long positions, but validate signals with additional analysis.

6.2 Setting Stop-Loss and Take-Profit Levels

Risk management is integral to successful trading. When employing MACD strategies, setting appropriate stop-loss and take-profit levels is crucial to protect capital and optimize returns.

- **Stop-Loss Strategies:**

  - **Based on Price Action:** Place stop-loss orders below/above key support/resistance levels identified on the price chart.

- **Volatility Adjustments:** Adjust stop-loss levels based on market volatility, using tools such as ATR (Average True Range).

- **Take-Profit Strategies:**

  - **Based on Trend Reversal Signals:** Consider taking profits when MACD signals suggest a potential trend reversal.

  - **Targeting Key Levels:** Identify key levels of support/resistance or Fibonacci retracement levels as potential take-profit points.

Balancing risk and reward is essential, and traders should adapt stop-loss and take-profit levels based on the specific characteristics of each trade and the overall market conditions.

6.3 Adapting MACD to Different Market Conditions

Market conditions are dynamic, and the efficacy of MACD strategies can vary. Traders need to adapt their approach based on the prevailing market environment.

- **Trending Markets:**

  - In strong trends, focus on MACD crossovers and trend confirmation signals.

  - Allow winning trades to run by trailing stop-loss levels along with the MACD.

- **Sideways or Range-Bound Markets:**

    - In choppy markets, use MACD to identify potential reversals at support/resistance levels.

    - Be cautious of false signals and consider shorter timeframes for more responsive signals.

- **Volatility Expansion or Contraction:**

    - Adjust MACD settings or use additional indicators to accommodate changing volatility.

    - Be aware of potential breakouts or breakdowns during periods of volatility expansion.

By adapting MACD strategies to different market conditions, traders can enhance their ability to generate consistent profits while minimizing losses.

In the following chapters, we will delve deeper into specific case studies, providing a more detailed understanding of how to apply MACD in various trading scenarios.

CHAPTER 7: PITFALLS AND CHALLENGES

7.1 False Signals and Whipsaws

While the Moving Average Convergence Divergence (MACD) indicator is a powerful tool, it is not immune to generating false signals and whipsaws. Traders must be aware of the following pitfalls:

- **Market Noise:** During periods of low volatility or when the market is range-bound, MACD signals can be misleading, resulting in false buy or sell indications.

- **Whipsaws:** Rapid and unexpected market reversals can lead to whipsaws, where the MACD generates a signal, only for the trend to reverse shortly afterward. This can result in losses for traders who act on premature signals.

Mitigation Strategies:

- **Confirmation Indicators:** Use additional technical indicators, such as trendlines, support/resistance levels, or other oscillators, to validate MACD signals.

- **Adjusting Timeframes:** Consider using shorter timeframes to reduce sensitivity to market noise, although this may sacrifice some signal accuracy.

7.2 Over-Reliance on MACD

Over-reliance on any single indicator can lead to biased decision-making and increased vulnerability to market fluctuations. Traders should be cautious not to rely solely on MACD and consider a holistic approach to technical analysis.

- **Confirmation from Other Indicators:** Utilize complementary indicators like Relative Strength Index (RSI), Moving Averages, or Bollinger Bands to cross-verify signals.

- **Incorporate Fundamental Analysis:** Consider macroeconomic factors, earnings reports, and news events to provide a broader context for trading decisions.

- **Historical Backtesting:** Assess the historical performance of MACD signals in the specific market and timeframe of interest. This helps gauge the reliability of the indicator in different scenarios.

7.3 Adapting to Changing Market Dynamics

Market conditions evolve over time, and traders must adapt their strategies to remain effective. What works well in a trending market may not perform as effectively during periods of consolidation or high volatility.

- **Changing Volatility:** Adjust MACD settings or incorporate volatility-based indicators to account for changing market conditions.

- **Sideways Markets:** During range-bound markets, consider using range-based strategies or adopting a mean-reverting approach.

- **Economic Events:** Be mindful of economic events, earnings releases, or geopolitical developments that can influence market dynamics. Adapt strategies accordingly to mitigate potential risks.

Remaining vigilant and adaptable is crucial for long-term success. Regularly reassess and refine trading strategies to align with the current market environment.

In the subsequent chapters, we will explore techniques for optimizing MACD strategies, addressing these challenges, and incorporating risk management principles for sustained success in the dynamic world of trading.

CHAPTER 8: MACD IN CRYPTOCURRENCY TRADING

8.1 Applying MACD to Cryptocurrencies

Cryptocurrency markets present unique challenges and opportunities, and the Moving Average Convergence Divergence (MACD) indicator can be a valuable tool in navigating this dynamic landscape.

- **Volatility in Crypto Markets:**

    - Cryptocurrencies are known for their inherent volatility. MACD, with its ability to capture momentum, is well-suited to identifying potential trends in the crypto space.

- **24/7 Trading:**

    - Unlike traditional financial markets that have specific trading hours, cryptocurrencies trade

24/7. This continuous market activity can lead to frequent MACD signals, requiring traders to adapt their strategies for more responsive decision-making.

- **Diverse Range of Assets:**

  - Cryptocurrencies come in various forms, from established ones like Bitcoin and Ethereum to countless altcoins. Each may have unique market behavior, and MACD can help traders analyze their individual trends.

8.2 Unique Challenges and Opportunities

- **Liquidity Concerns:**

  - Some cryptocurrencies may suffer from lower liquidity, leading to potential issues like slippage. Traders should exercise caution, especially in less-traded assets.

- **Market Sentiment Impact:**

  - Cryptocurrency prices can be influenced by sentiment and news in a more pronounced way than traditional markets. Traders should consider incorporating sentiment analysis alongside MACD for a comprehensive view.

- **Regulatory Changes:**

- The regulatory landscape for cryptocurrencies is evolving. MACD signals should be considered in the context of potential regulatory developments, which can significantly impact market dynamics.

8.3 Case Studies in Crypto Markets

- **Bitcoin Bull Run (2017):**

  - **Scenario:** During the Bitcoin bull run in 2017, the MACD provided numerous bullish crossovers.

  - **Action:** Traders might have considered entering long positions based on these crossovers.

  - **Outcome:** Successful trades as Bitcoin reached new all-time highs. However, caution was necessary to avoid the subsequent correction.

- **Altcoin Season (2021):**

  - **Scenario:** During the altcoin season in 2021, when many alternative cryptocurrencies experienced significant price surges, MACD crossovers and divergence patterns were prevalent.

  - **Action:** Traders could have used MACD signals to identify potential opportunities in various altcoins.

- **Outcome:** Profitability for those who accurately timed their entries and exits.

In cryptocurrency trading, MACD can be a versatile tool for identifying trends and potential reversal points. However, traders must remain vigilant due to the unique challenges presented by the crypto market.

In the upcoming chapters, we will explore more advanced strategies for cryptocurrency trading, incorporating MACD with other indicators and addressing the specific nuances of the digital asset space.

CHAPTER 9: BACKTESTING AND OPTIMIZATION

9.1 Importance of Backtesting

Backtesting is a crucial step in the development and refinement of any trading strategy, including those involving the Moving Average Convergence Divergence (MACD) indicator. Backtesting involves testing a trading strategy on historical market data to evaluate its performance and robustness. The importance of backtesting includes:

- **Performance Evaluation:** Backtesting allows traders to assess how a strategy would have performed in past market conditions. This insight helps gauge the strategy's potential effectiveness.

- **Risk Assessment:** Backtesting helps identify potential risks and drawbacks of a trading strategy, allowing traders to implement risk management measures accordingly.

- **Parameter Optimization:** By backtesting with different parameters, traders can optimize the settings of the MACD indicator for specific markets and timeframes.

9.2 Optimizing MACD Parameters

Optimizing MACD parameters involves finding the most suitable settings for the indicator based on historical data. While the default settings (12, 26, 9) are commonly used, market conditions may require adjustments. Key aspects to consider during optimization include:

- **Sensitivity to Trends:** Shortening the EMA periods (e.g., 5, 13, 5) increases the sensitivity of MACD to short-term trends, potentially providing more timely signals in fast-moving markets.

- **Reducing Noise:** Lengthening the EMA periods (e.g., 21, 55, 14) may reduce sensitivity to short-term fluctuations, offering more reliable signals in choppy or ranging markets.

- **Adapting to Asset Characteristics:** Different assets may require different MACD settings. For example, cryptocurrencies with high volatility might benefit from shorter EMA periods.

9.3 Using Backtest Results to Improve Strategies

After conducting backtests with various MACD settings, traders should analyze the results to refine and improve their strategies:

- **Identify Optimal Settings:** Look for parameter combinations that produced the best risk-adjusted returns during backtesting.

- **Understand Drawdowns:** Analyze periods of drawdown and losses to determine how well the strategy might withstand adverse market conditions.

- **Consider Transaction Costs:** Factor in transaction costs during backtesting to ensure the strategy remains viable in real-world trading scenarios.

- **Avoid Overfitting:** Be cautious of over-optimizing the strategy for historical data, as this may lead to poor performance in live markets.

Backtesting is an iterative process, and traders should continuously refine their strategies based on market changes and new data. While historical performance is not indicative of future results, thorough backtesting increases the likelihood of deploying robust and reliable trading strategies.

In the subsequent chapters, we will explore more advanced techniques, including the integration of machine learning and artificial intelligence with MACD, to further enhance trading strategies.

CHAPTER 10: PSYCHOLOGICAL ASPECTS OF MACD TRADING

10.1 Maintaining Emotional Discipline

Successful trading with the Moving Average Convergence Divergence (MACD) involves not only technical proficiency but also emotional discipline. The psychological aspects of trading play a crucial role in decision-making and overall performance.

- **Stick to the Plan:**

  - Develop a trading plan that incorporates MACD strategies, and adhere to it consistently. Emotional discipline involves avoiding impulsive decisions based on short-term market fluctuations.

- **Patience in Execution:**

- MACD signals may not always result in immediate market movements. Patience is essential to allow trades to unfold according to the strategy.

- **Avoiding FOMO and Panic:**

  - Fear of missing out (FOMO) can lead to impulsive entries, while panic may result in premature exits. MACD signals should be trusted within the context of the overall trading plan.

10.2 Dealing with Losses and Drawdowns

Losses are an inevitable part of trading, and the ability to handle them is critical for long-term success with MACD strategies.

- **Risk Management:**

  - Set clear risk limits and adhere to them rigorously. Avoid risking more than a predetermined percentage of your trading capital on a single trade.

- **Analyzing Losses Objectively:**

  - Instead of viewing losses as failures, treat them as opportunities to learn. Analyze losing trades objectively, seeking insights for improvement.

- **Drawdown Recovery:**

- During periods of drawdown, maintain composure and stick to the trading plan. Avoid chasing losses or deviating from the strategy.

10.3 Long-term Success with MACD

Achieving long-term success with MACD involves a combination of technical competence and psychological resilience.

- **Continuous Learning:**
  - Stay informed about changes in market conditions, new developments in technical analysis, and potential adjustments to MACD strategies.

- **Adaptability:**
  - Markets evolve, and successful traders must adapt. Regularly reassess MACD strategies in light of changing market dynamics.

- **Focus on Process, Not Outcome:**
  - Emphasize following a robust trading process over short-term gains. Success in trading is a marathon, not a sprint.

- **Embrace Consistency:**

- Consistent execution of proven MACD strategies, combined with disciplined risk management, is key to long-term success.

- **Mental Resilience:**

  - Trading can be emotionally challenging. Develop mental resilience to navigate the inevitable ups and downs without letting emotions dictate decisions.

By addressing the psychological aspects of trading, traders can enhance their ability to stick to their MACD strategies with discipline, weather losses, and pursue long-term success in the dynamic world of financial markets.

In the upcoming chapters, we will explore cutting-edge developments in trading, including the integration of artificial intelligence and machine learning with MACD, providing traders with advanced tools for their trading arsenal.

CHAPTER 11: FUTURE DEVELOPMENTS AND INNOVATIONS

11.1 Machine Learning and MACD

The synergy between machine learning (ML) and technical analysis, including the Moving Average Convergence Divergence (MACD) indicator, holds immense promise for the future of trading strategies.

- **Algorithmic Trading with MACD:**

    - Machine learning algorithms can analyze vast amounts of historical data to identify patterns and trends that may be challenging for humans to discern. This can enhance the effectiveness of MACD-based trading strategies.

- **Predictive Analytics:**

- ML models can be trained to predict future price movements based on MACD signals and other relevant indicators. This predictive capability can aid traders in making more informed decisions.

- **Adaptive Strategies:**

  - ML algorithms can continuously adapt MACD parameters based on current market conditions. This adaptability allows for more responsive strategies that evolve with changing trends.

11.2 Evolving Market Trends and MACD Adaptations

As financial markets continue to evolve, the adaptation of MACD strategies must align with emerging trends and technologies.

- **Cryptocurrency Integration:**

  - With the growing prominence of cryptocurrencies, MACD strategies will likely need adjustments to accommodate the unique characteristics of digital assets, such as 24/7 trading and heightened volatility.

- **Decentralized Finance (DeFi):**

  - The rise of DeFi platforms introduces new variables that can impact traditional technical analysis. MACD strategies may need to incorporate additional indicators or adapt to decentralized market dynamics.

- **Integration with Fundamental Data:**

  - Future developments may see increased integration of MACD with fundamental data, allowing traders to make more holistic and data-driven decisions.

11.3 The Future Landscape of Technical Analysis

The future landscape of technical analysis is likely to witness a fusion of traditional methods and cutting-edge technologies.

- **Integration of AI and Technical Analysis:**

  - Artificial intelligence will play an increasingly central role in technical analysis, aiding traders in processing vast datasets and making more informed decisions.

- **Quantum Computing Impact:**

  - As quantum computing capabilities advance, their application in financial markets could revolutionize the speed and complexity of technical analysis. MACD strategies may benefit from quicker and more intricate computations.

- **Enhanced Visualization Tools:**

- Future developments may bring about advanced visualization tools that provide traders with more intuitive and comprehensive displays of MACD signals and related data.

As technological advancements continue to reshape the financial landscape, traders and analysts must stay abreast of these changes. The fusion of MACD with machine learning and the adaptation of strategies to emerging market trends will be pivotal in navigating the evolving complexities of financial markets.

In the upcoming chapters, we will explore practical applications of these future developments, providing traders with insights and strategies to stay ahead in an ever-changing trading environment.

CHAPTER 12: CONCLUSION

12.1 Recap of Key Concepts

In this comprehensive guide, we've delved into the intricacies of the Moving Average Convergence Divergence (MACD) indicator and its application in trading. Let's recap the key concepts covered:

- **MACD Components:** The MACD comprises the MACD Line, Signal Line, and Histogram, each providing unique insights into market momentum.

- **Traditional MACD Strategies:** From basic crossovers to divergence patterns, we explored traditional strategies for leveraging MACD signals.

- **Advanced MACD Strategies:** We delved into advanced strategies, including interpreting MACD Histogram patterns, analyzing MACD slope and momentum, and combining MACD with other indicators.

- **Practical Application:** Real-world examples illustrated how to apply MACD in various market scenarios, set stop-loss and take-profit levels, and adapt to different market conditions.

- **Pitfalls and Challenges:** Understanding the potential pitfalls of false signals, over-reliance on MACD, and adapting to changing market dynamics is essential for successful trading.

- **MACD in Cryptocurrency Trading:** Explored the unique challenges and opportunities when applying MACD in the dynamic world of cryptocurrency trading.

- **Backtesting and Optimization:** Emphasized the importance of backtesting, optimizing MACD parameters, and using backtest results to improve trading strategies.

- **Psychological Aspects of MACD Trading:** Explored the importance of maintaining emotional discipline, dealing with losses and drawdowns, and achieving long-term success with MACD.

- **Future Developments and Innovations:** Discussed the potential integration of machine learning with MACD, adaptations to evolving market trends, and the future landscape of technical analysis.

12.2 Developing a Personalized MACD Trading Strategy

As you embark on your trading journey with MACD, consider developing a personalized strategy tailored to your risk tolerance, financial goals, and trading style. Here are key steps to guide you:

- **Define Your Goals:** Clearly outline your financial goals, whether they involve short-term gains, long-term investments, or a combination.

- **Understand Your Risk Tolerance:** Assess your risk tolerance and establish risk management parameters, including the percentage of capital to risk per trade.

- **Choose Appropriate Timeframes:** Select timeframes that align with your trading objectives, whether you're a day trader, swing trader, or long-term investor.

- **Optimize MACD Parameters:** Experiment with different MACD settings through backtesting to find the parameters that best suit your preferred markets and timeframes.

- **Incorporate Additional Indicators:** Consider integrating other technical indicators or fundamental analysis to enhance the robustness of your MACD strategy.

- **Stay Informed:** Regularly update your knowledge of market trends, economic developments, and changes in the financial landscape to adapt your strategy accordingly.

12.3 Continuing the Journey: Resources for Further Learning

The world of trading is dynamic, and continuous learning is paramount to success. Here are resources to deepen your understanding of MACD and trading:

- **Books:** Explore books on technical analysis, trading psychology, and algorithmic trading.

- **Online Courses:** Enroll in online courses covering technical analysis and trading strategies.

- **Financial News and Websites:** Stay updated with financial news and reputable websites that provide market analysis.

- **Professional Forums:** Join trading communities to share insights, learn from others, and stay informed about market trends.

- **Educational Platforms:** Utilize educational platforms that offer webinars, tutorials, and interactive learning experiences.

Remember, success in trading is a journey, not a destination. Continuously refine your skills, adapt to market changes, and stay disciplined in your approach. May your MACD strategies lead you to profitable and rewarding trading experiences. Happy trading!